LANGHAM
1940–1958

A Brief History including R.A.F. Weybourne

The publishing of this book would not have been possible without the initial research carried out by the late Len Bartram, of Hunworth. He produced the pamphlet that was the inspiration to the Friends of Langham Dome to reproduce his work and expand some of the sections. We are indebted to his widow, Evelyn, for allowing us to do so.

The picture on the front cover is a painting "Trouble Brewing" by the late Keith Aspinal. We are very grateful to his widow, Pat, for allowing us to reproduce it.

Books that were consulted for reference and checking were:
The Sky and I, by Veronica Volkersz
Dangerous Skies, by A.E.Clouston
Action Stations, by Mike Bowyer
Norfolk Crash Diaries, by Merv Hambling
Strike and Strike Again, by Ian Gordon
The Strike Wings, by Roy Conyers Nesbit

The photographs used in the book come from a variety of sources. We would particularly like to thank Richard Riding, former editor to Aeroplane Monthly, for many of them; David Jacklin and the Bircham Newton Memorial Project for delving into their archives and coming up with several Langham Photographs. We are very grateful to Richard Hoggett of the Norfolk County Council Historic Environment Service, who allowed us access to the 1946 aerial photographs of Langham and then allowed us to reproduce them for this book. Also to Dr Bert Osborn, former navigator in 455 Squadron RAAF, who supplied, amongst others, the incredible shots taken during intense moments of battle. He flew 25 missions from Langham and was one of the recipients of the Distinguished Flying Cross.

Produced for Friends of Langham Dome (FOLD) by Posthouse Publishing
www.posthousepublishing.com
First published in 2012
Reprinted with corrections 2014
Printed in Great Britain

CONTENTS

RAF Langham
1940–1958

At the beginning of the Second World War it was decided that most operational RAF airfields should have one or two smaller satellite bases available. These bases, often with just a grass landing strip, would be used for the dispersal of aircraft in event of enemy action, for training flights and for emergency use. Sites at Docking and Langham were chosen to serve as satellite bases for the Coastal Command airfield at Bircham Newton.

The site at Langham was first established early in 1940 on an area of farmland north of the Langham to Cockthorpe road. There were no buildings to begin with. The first airmen came from the parent station, Bircham, and numbered about twenty. They were billeted at Langham Hall in the village. The Hall also served as the Mess etc, during the early days. Not all local residents were happy about having an airfield near the village and stones were thrown at aircraft parked near the side of the Cockthorpe road, sometimes causing damage to Henley aircraft, so parking positions had to be changed. The first personnel included men to refuel and service the aircraft and to light and

maintain the night lighting which consisted of a Gooseneck flare path and a single Chance floodlight. There was also a fire crew, cooks and general duty workers. All supplies arrived each day by lorry from Bircham Newton.

Langham was a useful location in that it was close to the AA practice range at Weybourne on the north Norfolk coast. Target towing aircraft from Bircham operated daily for this range. Langham's first use was to refuel the Henley target tug aircraft and to provide for emergency landings if they had any problems, which they often did.

Blenheim Mk1/4s from Bircham were also dispersed here on a number of occasions during 1941. The grass field was also used by Hudsons from Bircham during 1940/42, especially for departing or returning from operations at night, the very primitive lighting at Langham being better than none at Bircham. On the night of 14 February 1941 a Blenheim, piloted by Squadron Leader Joseph Chamberlain of 235 Squadron was attempting to land at Langham when the flare path was suddenly extinguished due to enemy activity. The plane crashed at Croxton, near Fulmodeston. Chamberlain and the air gunner, Sergeant Owen Burns, were seriously injured, but the observer, P/O E.R. Phillips, was killed. He is buried in St. Mary's Church, Great Bircham.

Another early use of Langham in 1941/42 was that of a practice emergency landing field for Bomber Command Wellingtons which were on training flights.

LEFT: *A Lockheed Ventura loading 250lbs bombs. The Ventura, like the very similar Lockheed Hudson, was extensively used on maritime patrols.*

It is appropriate here to include a brief mention of RAF Bircham Newton, the parent station, which had overall control of Langham airfield until 1942.

Situated in northwest Norfolk about seven miles from the coast and five miles from Sandringham, it first opened as a Royal Flying Corps station in 1918. It was planned to be used as a base for heavy bomber raids on targets in Germany, but the war finished before these took place.

During 1920 the station was re-opened as a bomber base with DH-9s and Vimys. Many new buildings were built around this time and these remained in use until the station closed after the end of the Second World War.

The landing area was grass, with metal matting being added later. Public air displays were held annually during the 1930s.

The airfield was often used by aircraft of the King's Flight. During 1936 it was taken over for use by 16 Group Coastal Command RAF, in which role it served until the end of the Second World War.

A large number of different Coastal Command aircraft types and units operated from Bircham, several with Langham connections.

Docking was the other satellite airfield used by Bircham based squadrons. It also had many connections with Langham. By the end of 1941 a few buildings had been erected at Langham ready for the first RAF units to be permanently based there.

On 6 December 1941 'K' and 'M' Flights of No. 1 AACU (Anti-Aircraft Co-Operation Unit) arrived from Bircham Newton bringing twelve Hawker Henleys, two Tiger Moths, one Lysander and about two hundred personnel.

At first the only protection for the aircraft and any men working on them were engine tents - just a metal frame which was covered with canvas and placed over the nose of the aircraft. A flameless heater was placed in these tents on frosty nights, but they often went out and sometimes the tent itself was blown away.

The bitterly cold conditions of a north Norfolk winter was something well remembered by many of the airmen who were based at Langham.

During 1942 two or three Blister hangars were built on the north side of the strip for use in servicing the aircraft.

The Hawker Henley had been designed before the war to replace existing biplanes as a two seat light day bomber suitable for use as a dive bomber. It first flew in March 1937, but the Fairey Battle fulfilled the requirement and was ordered instead, so the Henley was relegated to the task of target towing duties.

Two hundred were then built for this role. It was a single engine two seat low wing monoplane very much like the Hurricane in appearance; in fact it used the same wings. Its engine was a

RIGHT: *A Hawker Henley. A two seater dive bomber. Not very successful so relegated to Target Tug.*

Rolls Royce Merlin of various marks. Usually old reconditioned engines were fitted to the aircraft at Langham. There were a number of problems with the engines and several aircraft had to make forced landings in the area due to engine trouble.

Three flag targets could be carried in the internal bomb bay. These were 30 feet long when unfurled and 5½ feet wide. Seven pounds of lead weights held them steady. The type mainly used was all red in colour. A wind driven winch was mounted outside below the rear cockpit and the drum held 7,000 feet of cable.

The winch operator occupied the rear cockpit seat and was usually an RAF airframe rigger, probably an LAC. Target towing (TT) operations were flown with the rear cockpit cover left off as it was found that when opening it to work the winch, it often came adrift and blew away.

Small smoke bombs could be carried in racks under the wings, if required.

The Henleys towed daily for the nearby Weybourne Heavy Anti Aircraft (HAA) practice range. The aircraft could be seen by the locals, with the tiny dot of the target straddled by a line of black shell bursts, followed seconds later by the crump of the explosion.

The Langham based aircraft also towed for other ranges in East Anglia, such as the Light Anti Aircraft range at Stiffkey, and for air to air firing practice over the North Sea.

During 1942 four Boulton Paul Defiants were also used as target tugs by 'K' Flight. Occasionally Lysanders were also used.

The radio-controlled Queen Bee was also used as a target at Weybourne. For test flights and transits these could be flown by a pilot and were sometime visitors to Langham. (See separate section in book.)

The Langham TT pilots were a very mixed bunch, comprising many foreign air force pilots hopeful of joining the RAF as operational air crew. Many were Poles who could not speak any English; several had flown in combat over Poland. In 1939 one senior Polish Air Force pilot (F/O Strojecki) had over 10,000 flying hours to his credit. Other ex-PAF pilots included Sgts. Pietrzak, Tomowicz, Mikusek, Czachia and Czapinski, who was sadly killed in a crash on Kelling Heath.

Other pilots included RAF men ill or injured and resting from operations and others waiting for courses or postings, etc.

The No. 1 AACU aircraft code letters when carried were '1' for 1 AACU, 'M' or 'K' for the Flight and the individual aircraft radio call sign letter i.e. 1M-A aircraft A of M Flt.

Flight Commanders were F/Lt Ashton and Davies.

On 9 November 1942 both 'M' and 'K' Flights were disbanded at Langham and immediately reformed as No. 1611 and 1612 TT

RIGHT: *A Boulton and Paul Defiant made in Wolverhampton. This was unsuccessful as a 'day' fighter plane and so was relegated to night fighter duties.*

Flights. Within a few days they had moved to Bircham Newton.

On 17 July 1942 six Swordfish biplane aircraft from 819 Squadron Fleet Air Arm arrived from Scotland. Painted black overall for night operations, with a crew of two, the third seat was occupied by an extra fuel tank which enabled the aircraft to reach the Dutch coast for mine laying operations. The Swordfish serial numbers were W5641/M, W5914/G, W5915/F, W5916/A, DK698/B and DK760/C.

Langham was now an independent station and had its first Commanding Officer, G/Capt. T.H. Carr DFC.

The first WAAF personnel arrived and were billeted at Cockthorpe Hall where they were often awakened by the loud footsteps of the resident ghost (or was it a size 9 RAF boot?)

Buildings on some of the sites in the village were ready and so on 5 August 1942 No. 280 Squadron moved in from Bircham, bringing with it fourteen Anson Mk 1s. Their duties were coastal patrols, reconnaissance and air sea rescue.

Other units which used the grass airfield before it closed included Army Co-Operation Mustang Mk 1s from No. 2 Squadron and P-40 Tomahawks from No. 231 Squadron, these aircraft taking part in Army manoeuvres in north Norfolk.

Wellingtons from No. 221 Squadron Bircham flew their night training exercises and night operations from Langham during this period. Other Wellingtons from a Polish squadron planned to bomb Berlin flying from Langham, probably because it was the nearest base to the German capital, but with a full fuel and bomb load on board the grass runway was too short for the aircraft to get airborne, so after a number of the aircraft had aborted the take off, the operation was abandoned.

Because of its proximity to the Ack-Ack ranges Langham's use as a diversion airfield was limited.

Visiting aircraft were mainly connected with the AACU or the Army at Weybourne.

In November 1942 the airfield was closed for extension and the laying of concrete runways.

Army and RAF regiments remained at the base for security and training purposes.

The New Airfield

During the time the airfield was closed for reconstruction work, No. 1626 Flight, a small RAF unit, operated from the grass on the north edge of site, equipped with Lysander aircraft. The actual duties of this flight are uncertain; they might have been target towing or other Army Co-Op. work. Rumours have suggested

RIGHT: *A Fairey Swordfish nicknamed the 'String Bag' and entered service in July 1936. It became famous due to its involvement in the sinking of the Bismarck.*

that on occasions Lysanders did use Langham as a base for Special Duty operations to Holland.

The airfield re-opened on 1 March 1944 as an independent operational station in No. 16 Group RAF Coastal Command. Group Capt. A.E. Clouston DSO DFC AFC was appointed Station Commander. At this time work was still in progress and the runways were not ready to receive any aircraft.

Group Capt. A.E. Clouston, DSO DFC AFC Commander, Langham Airfield, March 1944 to May 1945

Group Captain Clouston was well experienced in Coastal Command operations when he was posted to command Langham, having previously been Commanding Officer of No. 224 (Leigh Light) B-24 Liberator Squadron. He had been one of the Leigh Light pioneers and had done much of the early flight testing.

The Leigh Light was an airborne searchlight used mainly to illuminate enemy submarines.

Clouston got on particularly well with the Australian and New Zealand personnel. He was well respected by all ranks for his fairness to all. He organised the station farming enterprise, and, being a keen sportsman, he arranged regular hare and rabbit shoots on the airfield; the bag he gave to the airmen and civilian workers whom he considered needed it most.

Piano smashing contests between different units was another sport he supported and he gave full backing to the station bands and concert party.

He had his own private aircraft which he kept at Langham, probably a DH Moth Minor G-AFPR, but some reports suggest it was an all blue pre-war Miles monoplane. He had his own US Jeep given to him by a USAAF squadron.

Arthur Clouston was born in New Zealand in 1908, the son of a gold miner. His quest for flying brought him to England to join the RAF. He passed out with top marks as a pilot and was posted to No. 25 Fighter Squadron. He soon became their chief display pilot and performed at Hendon air shows during the 1930s. At Farnborough he flew test flights for many new types of aircraft; other work there included the deliberate flying of aircraft into barrage balloon cables!

He became part owner of a DH 88 Comet G-ACSS and set distance and air speed records to and from New Zealand and South Africa.

He also competed in many air sporting events including the King's Cup and Schlesinger air races.

It was said he had experience of flying more different types of aircraft and had more flying hours than virtually any other pilot during his time of service.

Group Captain Clouston, a keen country sportsman, formed a good relationship with local land owners who helped him to set up a pig, poultry and vegetable growing enterprise on the base, the produce going to supplement the camp rations for all ranks. A gang of Italian POWs helped with this work.

On VE Day at a mass meeting at Langham, he thanked all the aircrew, airmen and WAAFs who had served there under his command. Soon after, he was posted to serve with the RAF in occupied Germany, later commanding the test pilots' school at Farnborough and the test establishment at Boscombe Down.

Retiring with the rank of Air-Commodore, he died at his home in Cornwall in 1984.

Description of the New Layout

Three concrete runways were laid in the familiar 'A' war time pattern. The longest main runway SW/NE was 2,000 yards long, the other two were shorter, but all were 50 yards wide and all were linked by a concrete perimeter taxi track. Alongside the perimeter track were 36 concrete aircraft dispersal parking points.

This work made it necessary to close the Langham/Cockthorpe public road. Three T2 type hangars were built, two on the main technical site and one on the north (Cockthorpe) side.

Some of the old blister hangars - there had been four - were left standing for a while.

The technical site contained the Squadron offices, crew rooms, MT section, armoury, workshops, stores, parachute section, dinghy shed, fuel installation and also rather less common buildings like the underground battle HQ, the bombing trainer building and the Dome teacher building – more about this building, and its use, later in the book.

The bomb store site was on the north (Morston) side. The communal, WAAF and all other billet sites were situated in and around Langham village.

On the airfield in front of the technical site was the flying control building (Watch Office type 12779/41), which, I believe, was built earlier. This building is still standing at the time of publication (2012) and is used as an office and stores by Bernard Matthews PLC.

OVERLEAF LEFT AND RIGHT: *1946 aerial photographs of the airfield.*

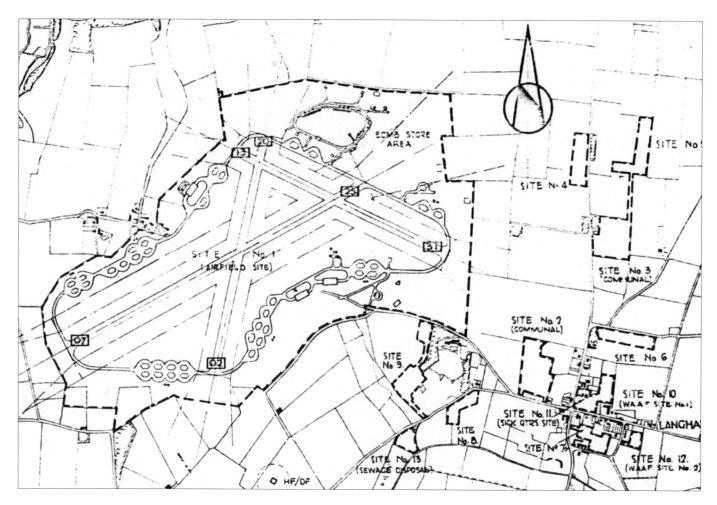

BOMB STORE AREA

SITE No

SITE No. 4

SITE No. 3
(COMMUNAL)

SITE No. 1
(AIRFIELD SITE)

SITE No. 2
(COMMUNAL)

SITE No 6

SITE No 9

SITE No 10
(WAAF SITE No.1)

SITE No. 11
(SICK QTRS SITE)

SITE No. 12
(WAAF SITE No. 2)

LANGHA

SITE No 7

SITE No. 8

SITE No. 13
(SEWAGE DISPOSAL)

HF/DF

20

13

25

31

07

02

16

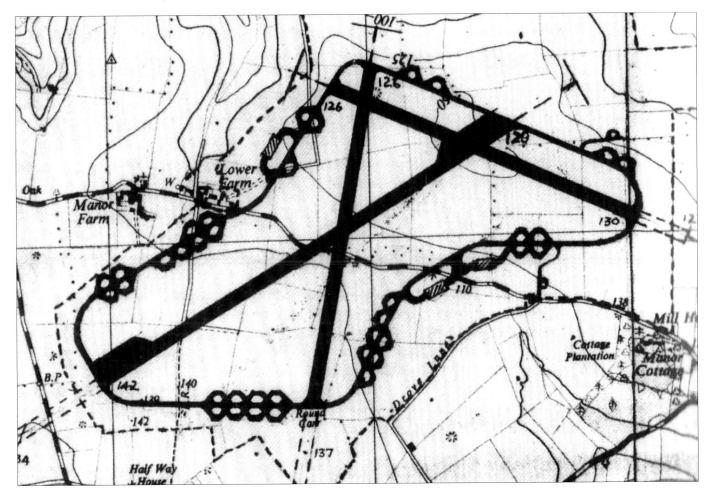

The Squadrons

No 455 Royal Australian Air Force and No 489 Royal New Zealand Air Force sqdns

Known as the ANZAC Wing, they arrived from Leuchars during the week 6/12 April 1944, equipped with Beaufighter Mk TF10s. These squadrons were to form the Langham Strike Wing which was to operate in the anti-shipping role. Some aircraft would carry torpedoes (Torbeaus), others rockets (Flakbeaus). Bombs could also be carried, plus all aircraft carried the normal armament of cannons.

These aircraft were soon in action attacking convoys, supply ships, flak ships, E and R-Boats and midget submarines off the Dutch, German and Southern Norwegian coasts, and later supporting the D-Day landing forces. These air/sea battles, at close quarters, were ferocious. Casualties were appallingly heavy on both sides, but the effect on the German war effort was immense, severely restricting any ship movements along the German, Dutch, French and Norwegian coasts. During those hectic few months, these two Langham Squadrons sank over 30 enemy ships, damaged another 60 or so, and sank 4 U-boats .

PREVIOUS PAGES LEFT AND RIGHT: *1946 aerial maps of the airfield.*

FACING PAGE: *455 Squadron Royal Australian Air Force.*

On occasions the two squadrons would team up with other aircraft from North Coates, in Lincolnshire, and form a 'Strike Wing' of up to seventy-two Beaufighters.

Mustangs and Spitfires, from RAF Coltishall, would, occasionally, provide fighter escort for the Beaufighter attacks, and at dusk Wellingtons would drop flares to assist.

The Commanding Officer of 455 sqdn was W/Cdr J Davenport DSO, DFC and Bar, GM, and of 489 sqdn W/Cdr J.S. Dinsdale DSO.DFC. and from August 1944 W/Cdr Robertson.

By October 1944, day time movements of enemy shipping had been reduced to such an extent, and Wellingtons could cope with night time action, that 455 and 489 sqdns moved back to Scotland to continue to harass shipping in northern waters off Norway.

The courage of these pilots and navigators cannot be under estimated, twenty two members of **489 Squadron** lost their lives in the six months they flew from Langham. Perhaps an indication can also be gained by appreciating the number of decorations awarded.

During the period of January 1944 and May 1945 the following decorations were awarded to:

455 Squadron	489 Squadron
2 x George Medals	--
1 x Bar to Distinguished Service Order (DSO)	--

455 Squadron	489 Squadron
3 x DSO	2 x DSO
5 x Bar to Distinguished Flying Cross (DFC)	1 x Bar to DFC
25 x DFC	19 DFC
1 x Distinguished Flying Medal	1 x Conspicious Gallantry Medal

No. 280 Squadron

During August 1944 280 Squadron returned to Langham, now equipped with Warwick Air Sea Rescue Mk 1s. These aircraft could carry a large airborne lifeboat which, if needed, could be dropped attached to a number of parachutes. Their main role was to give ASR (Air Sea Rescue) support for the Arnhem airborne invasion, after which they moved to Beccles, Suffolk.

No. 2820 Squadron RAF Regiment

2820 Squadron, which had been responsible for the airfield defence, left Langham on 28 July 1944.

Air attacks upon the base were few in number, the most

memorable being on 20 March 1945 when anti-personnel bombs were dropped, killing some cattle in fields between Langham and Binham.

No. 612 Squadron

612 Squadron moved to Langham on 18 December 1944 from Limavardy, Londonderry, where they had been engaged on anti-submarine operations.

The Commanding Officer was W/Cdr. D.M. Brass who was replaced in February 1945 by W/Cdr. A..M. Taylor who, due to sickness, was then replaced by W/Cdr. G. Henderson.

612 Ground Servicing Echelon occupied the hangar nearest to the flying control tower.

On 18 March 1945 a ground explosion destroyed two aircraft. Prompt action by ground staff prevented further loss.

F/Lt. Jeff Rounce, a 612 Squadron Wellington pilot, was lucky, as he lived locally.

Their aircraft were Wellington GR 14s, in Coastal Command white. A crew of six was carried. At Langham many of their operations were night anti-shipping patrols using the latest mark of ASV radar. Their patrol area stretched from the Dutch coast to the Baltic, E-boats being one of the targets sought, but many successful attacks were made on enemy shipping of all sizes. The Squadron

LEFT: *489 Squadron Royal New Zealand Airforce.*

455 and 489 Squadron going into attack

ABOVE: *Attack in progress. A chaotic scene of swirling aircraft going into attack.*

ABOVE: *Into Battle: Note the barrage balloon attached to the ship being attacked and the trail of a rocket fired from the ship at the attacking aircraft.*

was highly commended on its duties carried out from Langham.

The Squadron was disbanded at Langham on 9 July 1945. Pre-war it had been The County of Aberdeen Royal Auxiliary Air Force Squadron.

Brief Examples of 612 Anti-Shipping Operations

21 March 1945: Wellington NB877/M
F/O. D.R. Morgan, sighted 8 E-boats, attacked, but bombs failed to release until the third run resulting in a near miss on one boat. Intense, light flak experienced.

21 March 1945: Wellington NC800/J
P/O. F.G. Duff, shadowed and attacked 4 E-boats; bombs straddled wake, very heavy flak.

22 March 1945: Wellington NC800/J
F/Lt. J. Dewhurst, sighted 5 E-boats, shadowed and sent report to Royal Navy Frigates, who engaged, and drove off enemy boats, continued to shadow, attacked, bombs straddled 3 boats, intense flak.

22 March 1945: Wellington NC420/O
F/Lt. J.H. Johnson, shadowed radar contacts, developed engine trouble but attacked, hit by flak, forced to ditch, all crew picked up midday 23rd by Catalina, one crew member broken arm, others O.K.

25 March 1945: Wellington NC797/P
F/Lt. W.A. Cormack, attacked 4 E-boats through intense accurate flak, bombs burst near the leading boat, 2 enemy aircraft seen circling boats.

25 March 1945: Wellington ND133/A
F/Sgt. D.R. Owen, attacked 4 E-boats in face of intense flak and rockets, near miss on boat crashed on landing at base in zero visibility, crew unhurt but aircraft was destroyed.

Some other 612 pilots at this time were:
S/Ldr. S.R. Kendal, F/Lt. R.E. Priest (RNZAF), F/Lt. N.P. Ramsey, F/Lt. J.N.B. Rounce DFC, F/O. J.H. Smith, F/O. W.F. Wood (RAAF), F/O. D.L. Mumford, P/O. W.C. Monckton, and P/O. D.N. Goddard.

No. 407 (RCAF) Squadron
Wellington GR14s (Leigh Light) from 407 Squadron arrived at Langham from Chivenor just prior to the end of the war. Their final patrol was carried out on VE night, their role being to curb any last minute German Navy action.

No. 524 Squadron
524 Squadron was first formed on 20 October 1943 to evaluate and operate the Martin Mariner flying boat, a large and impressive looking U.S. Navy twin engine patrol boat PBM-3 of a type very rarely seen in this country. In fact, those which were received by 524 Squadron at Oban were returned to the USA after a couple of months, for reasons unknown!

524 Squadron was reformed at Davidstow Moor on 7 April 1944 as a Coastal Command unit flying the Wellington GR13, the crews having formed up at Haverford West OTU a few days earlier.

The Commanding Officer was Sqdn/Ldr. A.W. Naismith. By the end of the month the Squadron commenced operations against E-boats and other enemy shipping. During June anti-shipping support was given to the Allied invasion forces.

With the area of its operations moving to Belgium and Dutch coasts the Squadron moved to Docking, Norfolk on 1st July 1944. Here it took over aircraft and crews of 415 (RCAF) Squadron, giving it a total now of 16 Wellingtons. On 13 July 1944 W/Cdr. R.G. (Knotty) Knot DFC assumed command of the Squadron.

Due to lack of space at Docking, the 524 HQ and ground servicing section moved to Bircham Newton. Airfields along the south coast were used as a base for any operations which were still sometimes made along the north west coast of France, and later a detachment was based at Dallachy, Scotland for special operations.

Another problem at Docking was the water logging of the grass airfield after heavy rain. When this occurred, some of the

THIS PAGE: *Loading a Beaufighter with a torpedo. The Beaufighter was powered by twin 1400hp Bristol Hercules XI engines.*
FACING PAGE: *A Bristol Beaufighter firing rockets.*

ABOVE AND RIGHT: *A Vickers Warwick with under-slung lifeboat, designed by Uffa Fox, for dropping to ditched crew.*

flying was done from Langham. Later, aircraft were deployed to Langham on a temporary basis, but on 18 October 1944 the squadron moved to Langham from Docking, followed on 1 November 1944 by the HQ and servicing staff from Bircham.

524 Squadron occupied the hangar in front of the technical site with the dispersals on the south side of the airfield.

Its main role was, like 612 Squadron, anti-shipping patrols along the enemy coastline. Shipping of all types, from midget subs and E-boats to large supply ships, were attacked on sight or by radar contact.

Flares and 500lb bombs were carried. AA fire from the ships and supporting flak ships was often very severe and a number of aircraft were lost; sometimes enemy fighters were also encountered. Three 524 aircrew were killed in a crash at Langham on 26 March 1945, and two Warrant Officers were killed in a local road accident on 10 March 1945.

Well remembered on the squadron was The Hon. F/Lt. (Grimmy) Grimston, said to be from a titled family. He was respected and well liked by all ranks and trades, including the ground crews to whom he handed out fags and told them about the operations carried out.

He was sadly missed when he failed to return from an operation flown from Docking. In his memory a Wellington on the Squadron was named "Grimmy's Revenge".

The 524 Squadron Wellingtons were painted black overall, an unusual colour for Coastal Command aircraft, the reason being that the Squadron was mainly intended for operations at night.

Many of the Squadron's patrol operations are recorded by code names only, such as Box Patrol, Crossover Patrol, Percolate and Ashfield.

During the winter of 1944/45 detachments operated from Dallachy, Scotland. Operations continued daily from Langham up to 4 May 1945. On 5 May orders were given for the Squadron to move immediately to Wick in the north of Scotland. It was suspected that the Germans might attempt a last ditch stand in Norway.

With everything packed ready to move and the aircraft on the point of taking off, the move was cancelled.

The next morning, 8 May 1945, the station duty crew went around the billets and woke up the airmen with the news "The war's over!" The ground staff cycled to work as usual, where on arrival they were told report to the control tower where announcements and a thanksgiving service took place.

A party and other celebrations were held on 12 May 1945, which were followed over the next few days by sightseeing flights for ground staff along the Dutch and German coasts. On 24 May 1945 the AOC visited to thank all personnel and also to inform them that the Squadron would be disbanded the very next day.

ABOVE: *Fl/Sgt John Saul's crew. Back row left to right: Fl/Sgt Peter Brewster, Fl/Sgt H.Hoyer Fl/sgt J.Church. Front row L to R: Fl/Sgt John Saul, W O Jack Royers, Fl/Sgt W.Bates.*
RIGHT: *612 Squadron, 1st August 1945.*

No. 521 Meteorological Squadron

521 Meteorological Squadron was formed at Bircham Newton on 1 August 1942 from 1401 Meteorological Flight. On 31 March 1943 the Squadron was split into two flights, 1401 and 1409. On 1 September 1943 521 was reformed as a squadron once again, but now at Docking, where it remained for twelve months until 30 October 1944 when it moved to Langham, taking over the hangar and dispersals on the north (Cockthorpe) side of the base.

The Squadron used a wide variety of aircraft types depending

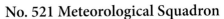

ABOVE: *524 Squadron. Wellington crew.*
TOP RIGHT: *521 Squadron. In front of a Flying Fortress — B17.*

on what could be spared from operational needs. Nevertheless the importance of the work done by the Squadron should not be overlooked since the final decision about whether operations were on or scrubbed often depended on reports from the Meteorological Squadrons.

There were daily flights of the Squadron's old Gladiators from Langham. They would climb up over north Norfolk to take barometer readings. Venturas operated over the North Sea and Europe and later ex-Coastal Command Fortress GR2s flew sorties to Norway and out into the Atlantic. Hurricanes took over from the Gladiators; some of these remained at Langham as 1402 Flight after 521 Squadron left on 3 November 1945.

Squadrons and Other Units Based at Langham

248 Sqdn. Blenheim 4f. *Jun 41 to Dec 41 Detachment*
No. 1 AACU 'K' Flight. 1K. Henley TT 6 *Dec 41 to Nov 42*
No. 1 AACU 'M' Flight. 1M. Henley TT 6 *Dec 41 to Nov 42*
No. 1 AACU 'M' Flight. 1M. Defiant TT *August 42 to Oct 42*
819(FAA) Sqdn. Swordfish 17 *Jul 42 to 6 August 42*
280 Sqdn. YF. Anson 1 5 *August 42 to Nov 42*
231 Sqdn. VM. Tomahawk 1 *1942 Detachment*
2 Sqdn. XV. Mustang 1 *1942 Detachment*
143 Sqdn. HO. Beaufighter 1c *Jul/August 1942 Detachment*

FAR LEFT AND LEFT: *Flying Fortress of 521 Met Squadron.*

221 Sqdn. DF. Wellington GR8 *1942 Detachment*
206 Sqdn. VX. Hudson GR *1942 Detachment*
No. 1611 TT Flight. Henley TT *Nov 1942*
No. 1612 TT Flight. Henley TT *Nov 1942*
No. 1626 TT Flight. Lysander TT *Jul 43 to Nov 43*
254 Sqdn. QY. Beaufighter 6 *Oct 42 to Nov 42 Detachment*

Airfield re-construction work took place 1943/44

455 (RAAF) Sqdn. UB. Beaufighter TF10 12 *Apr 44 to Oct 44*
489 (RNZAF) Sqdn. P6. Beaufighter TF10 12 *Apr 44 to Oct 44*
280 Sqdn. MF. Warwick ASR1 6 *August 44 to Oct 44*
827 (FAA) Sqdn. Barracuda. 1 *Nov 44 to 13 Dec 44*
524 Sqdn. 7R. Wellington GR13 *Jul 44 to Oct 44 Detachment*
524 Sqdn. 7R. Wellington GR13 18 *Oct 44 to Dec 44*

524 Sqdn. 7R. Wellington GR14 *Dec 44 to 25 Jun 45*
612 Sqdn. 8W. Wellington GR14 18 *Dec 44 to 7 Jul 45*
407 (RCAF) Sqdn. Wellington GR14 *14 Apr 45 to 10 May 45*
521 (MET) Sqdn. Gladiator, Hurricane, Hudson, Ventura *Oct 44/Apr 45*
521(MET) Sqdn. Fortress GR2/3(Met) *Dec 44 to 3 Nov 45*
No. 1402(MET) Flight. DQ. Hurricane 2 *Dec 45 to May 46*
254 Sqdn. QM. Beaufighter TF10 Nov 45 to May 46
No. 1561/1562 (MET) Flights. Spitfires *Dec 45 to Feb 46*
MCF (Met Conversion Flight) *1945*
Station Flights. Tiger Moth etc. *1944/45*
No. 2 ATC (Armament Training Camp) Martinet *1944*
CCFATU. Martinet, Spitfire *Sep 45 to Jan 46*
Royal Netherlands Air Force. Tech Training School. *Jun 46/Sept 47*
43rd LAA/Searchlight Regiment RA *1947/51*
No. 2 CAACU. *Jul 52 to Oct 58*
US Army Radio Controlled Target Aircraft Detachment. *1951/57*
US Army Skysweeper AA Gun Training Unit *1953/57*
US Army E/W Radar Unit att. to 39AAA Batt. of 32AAA Brigade *1953/5*

LEFT: *Gloster Gladiators and crews. Delightful to fly but outclassed by later monoplane fighters.*
ABOVE: *Hawker Hurricane, Armed with four Hispano 20mm cannons.*

USAF Sculthorpe emergency landing runway *1960s*
British Army Stores Unit *1950s/60s*
Bernard Matthews PLC *1970s* -

Another unusual type of aircraft seen at Langham were Barracudas from No. 827 (FAA) Squadron which gave support to operations along the Dutch coast during November 1944.

The final RAF Squadron to occupy the base was No. 254 Squadron from November 1945 to May 1946 with Beaufighters. All flying ceased at the end of May 1945.

For one year from June 1946, the base was loaned to the Royal Netherlands Air Force for use as a technical training school until facilities were available in Holland.

The airfield was then closed and placed under care and maintenance.

FAR LEFT: *Spitfires. Probably mark V's. Armed with a cannon and machine gun on each wing.*
ABOVE: *Fairey Barracuda which entered service in late 1943 and powered by 1640hp Rolls Royce Merlin.*
LEFT: *Avro Anson. Known as 'Faithful Annie'. Used mainly by Coastal Command.*

Royal Netherlands Air Force Technical Training School

At the end of the war, it was not possible to organise training for a Netherlands Air Force in Holland itself. Holland had been plundered and there were not enough financial or technical resources to undertake the training required. It was therefore decided, in co-operation with the RAF, that Langham, with its now semi-redundant accommodation, offered just the place for a technical-military training school to be set up. In June 1946 several hundred Dutch servicemen took over the Nissan hut accommodation evacuated by the RAF personnel some months previously.

The staff and instructors were drawn from Dutch men who had served during the war in the RAF Squadrons 320, 321 and 322, as well as from recruits who had joined up having been liberated in 1944 and subsequently gone through a technical training instructor's course at RAF Cosford. There were also some RAF officers and NCOs to give further advice. The trainees, who came directly from the Netherlands, were war volunteers and conscripts from the Dutch Navy and Air Force.

Conditions were decidedly uncomfortable and, with one of the most severe winters to come, would get a lot worse. From January to March 1947, there was considerable snow; the village

was often cut off and the Dutch men found themselves digging the village out. With the lack of food, clothing and fuel to heat the huts, morale was very low. In the words of a young Dutch Air Force chaplain, Van der Poel, 'it was an appalling mess'. "There is almost nothing. London and Holland will not listen to us", he complained. A mutiny was narrowly averted by the Reverend Van der Poel and the arrival of an early, warm spring.

Over the years, though, most of those negative memories have been erased, and many have made the pilgrimage back to Langham in happier times. In 1997 a party of eighty made the journey back to mark the 50th anniversary. A formal reception in the village church was held, a plaque was dedicated, and much merriment was had in the Bluebell pub!

It has been suggested that without the skills learnt by those trainees at Langham during that period, there would be not have been a Royal Netherlands Air Force, KLM Airlines or Philips Electronics, as we know them today. Such was the level of training received at Langham that most of the trainees went onto have good careers in those organisations.

FAR LEFT TOP: *Aircraft Trainees from the Royal Dutch Fleet Air Arm*
LEFT: *Aircraft parked outside the Cockthorpe T-2 Hangar.*
ABOVE: *The snow in the winter of 1946/47 with inset showing the height of the snow against the signpost on the Holt Road/Blakeney Road T Junction.*

The Dome Trainer

In 1939 Henry Christian Stephens conceived the idea of projecting films of aircraft onto a curved wall to train anti-aircraft gunners. Having served in the Royal Navy during the First World War and been a midshipman aboard H.M.S. Milbrook at the Battle of Jutland, Stephens joined the Royal Navy Volunteer Reserve in order to develop his idea.

And so, working at the Royal Navy's School of Gunnery, HMS Excellent in Portsmouth, the Dome Trainer was born.

Having developed the system initially for Naval Gunners, the Army became interested in it for training gunners defending airfields.

About 46 concrete and steel Domes, of the Langham design were built during the war on airfields around the country. Only about six survive today.

So how did the Domes work?

A 35mm camera was positioned on a pair of concrete piers in the middle of the Dome. Through an ingenious use of movable mirrors and cams, the image of the aircraft from a film made by Technicolor could be projected onto the wall and moved to create a realistic image of an attacking aircraft. The trainee gunner was positioned behind the projector and mirrors at his replica gun – something like a twin Browning machine gun, Bofors or Lewis gun for light anti-aircraft gunnery training. When the gunner opened fire an amplifier produced the deafening rattle of the weapon being fired. The noise of the attacking aircraft was recorded on the soundtrack of the film. With these sound effects the pupil got a very realistic feeling of being attacked and having to respond. In order for the instructor to assess the accuracy of the pupil, a yellow dot was incorporated onto each frame of the film, showing the aircraft's future position and therefore where the gunner should be aiming. This yellow dot could be obscured from the pupil's vision by using a yellow filter on the gun site.

ABOVE RIGHT: *The Dome before renovation in 2012.*

As the pupil fired, a yellow image of the gun site was projected down the line of fire so the instructor could see whether this image coincided with the yellow dot of the future position of the aircraft, thus claiming a hit or miss!

Trainee gunners were put through their paces in the Dome before being allowed down to Stiffkey for a 'live' firing practice at drones towed by aircraft out over the marsh – obviously the 'powers that be' wanted to make sure the gunners were proficient enough not to shoot down the towing aircraft!

Late in the war, and possibly when the Americans were stationed at Langham in the early 1950s, the ground-to-air gun was replaced by a replica of an aircraft gun turret for air-to-air gunnery simulation. The training would have been very similar.

So what of the future for this rare building?

In January 2010, the local community set up the Friends of Langham Dome to work with North Norfolk Historic Buildings Trust, to whom Bernard Matthews PLC had donated the building, with the aim of raising enough money to renovate and repair it and to create an interpretation of its war time use. It was planned that it would then be available to the general public and to schools to tell the story of the important contribution made by Langham and other East Anglian airfields to the defence of this country during the Second World War. It was also intended that it would tell the history of RAF Langham itself so that it could become a memorial to those who served at Langham and particularly those that flew from the airfield and never made it back.

In 2013, substantial grants from the Heritage Lottery Fund, English Heritage and others, meant that the aims of The Friends of Langham Dome and the North Norfolk Historic Buildings Trust could be realised. Substantial work has been undertaken and Langham Dome opened as a visitor centre in July 2014.

If you would like to support the Dome, please join the Friends of Langham Dome. Details are available at **www.friendsoflanghamdome.org**.

43 Light Anti-Aircraft/Search Light Regiment, Royal Artillery

The Regiment arrived at Langham in late 1947, although the 84th Searchlight Regiment, who then amalgamated with the 43rd, may have been stationed here for a while before. The officers and men were billeted in rather basic huts, mostly Nissen huts. The officers' huts were beside Langham Hall, which was the Medical Reception Station (MRS), but they had to walk to the camp site down the Morston road to their Mess for meals. In 1950 the Mess was moved to buildings on what is now St. Mary's housing estate. The men's huts were dotted around the village in the old RAF camp sites.

The Commanding Officer was Lt.Col. John Gregson. He had been a Major General during the Second World War but had to revert to his substantive rank afterwards. The Commanding Officer's house was Home Close, in North Street.

The Regiment was equipped with 40mm Bofors guns and regularly trained in the Dome. The men would then go to Stiffkey for live firing against targets towed by various aircraft.

No. 2 CAACU (Civilian Anti-Aircraft Co-Operation Unit)

This unit, operated by Marshalls of Cambridge on a government contract, was formed during 1951 to take over Army Co-Operation duties in the Norfolk area from No. 34 Squadron RAF which was disbanded at Horsham St Faiths.

34 Squadron already had Langham connections going back to the No. 1 AACU of 1941. It had been renumbered from 695 Squadron, which in turn had originated from 1611/1612 Flights at Bircham.

The personnel of 2 CAACU were civilian but nearly all had served in the RAF; in fact, all pilots had to be members of the RAF Reserve or Auxiliary Air Force.

After the disbandment of 34 Squadron, its Spitfire LF16s moved to Little Snoring during August 1951 to form the new CAACU. Here the condition of the runways was so bad that the

ABOVE RIGHT: *De Havilland Vampire. First generation of jet fighter which came into service in 1948.*
RIGHT: *De Havilland Mosquitoes. Known as Mossies and the 'Wooden wonder'. Powered by twin Rolls Royce Merlin engines.*

Beaufighters could not operate from them and had to be based at Cambridge until permission to move to Langham was granted in 1952.

The manager of the unit was Mr Jeff Barkley. Senior Pilot was Mike Ingle-Finch DFC, an ex fighter pilot. Other pilots included Richard Younghusband, ex ATA and test pilot, Duggie Neal, Ronnie Temple-Harris, also ex-ATA, Dennis Turnbull, Taff Rich, Alan Blackwell, Stephan (Bostic) Wotjik (Polish), Anderson (Sweden) Deacon and Veronica Volkersz - a pilot with exceptional flying skill and experience, commencing pre-war with the CAA and as a ferry pilot with the ATA during the war, when she delivered hundreds of aircraft of many different types.

TTOs (Target Tow Operators) with the CAACU at Langham included Norman de-Gray, an ex-RAF pilot who lived at the old Horse Shoes public house in Stody village, Dick Butler and

David (Jack) Smith.

The role of the unit was target towing for the Heavy Ack-Ack Range at Weybourne and for a Light Ack-Ack Range nearby on Stiffkey marshes using Beaufighter TT10s, supplemented and eventually replaced by Mosquito TT35s.

Spitfires were used for Army gun laying, Army close air ground support and RAF radar calibration.

A fleet of Vampire FB5s, FB9s and T11 two seaters were added later to supplement the Spitfires. They would often be seen flying in line astern making mock low level attacks on troops at Weybourne, Kelling Heath, Plumstead Heath and Hempstead Woods. Oxfords were used for night searchlight exercises.

During 1958 the unit had up to 34 different aircraft in service at one time. Examples of aircraft that served at Langham included: Beaufighter SR911/G, RD767/E, Mosquito TT35 TA703/F, TA633/E, RV367/J, TH981/L, Oxford ED108/A, NM539/B, Anson T21 WB457/A, Spitfire TE203/M, TE257/P, SL713/S,

ABOVE: *Langham employees of Marshalls of Cambridge's School of Army Co-operation.*
LEFT: *De Havilland Dragoon Rapide and Spitfire outside T-2 Hangar. A Mosquito can be seen outside the far door.*

TB675/Z, Vampire FB5 WA124/L, VV687/R, VZ195/56, VX983/52, WA282/Z, FB9 WL573/47, WP994/54, WR113/57, T11 WZ584/41, XE869/42.

Visiting aircraft included Dragon Rapides from Marshalls, Mosquito T3 RAF from White Waltham, where pilot conversion to Mossies was carried out, and L-20 Beavers from the US Army and Air Force.

Sometimes the CAACU aircraft were called upon to take part in ROC and RAF air defence exercises. Defending jets were surprised when their foe turned out to be a Second World War Spitfire flown by Veronica with her long flowing blond hair!

On occasions pilots and aircraft from the CAACU took part in the making of films.

During 1958 the re-training of TA Ack-Ack personnel was coming to an end and the development of ground to air missiles for future air defence was well advanced. Together this meant the end for AA practice camps like Weybourne.

The last Army Co-Op. flight by 2 CAACU was made on 13 October 1958, and after an air defence exercise a few days later, the unit was closed down, the aircraft being flown out to an Maintenance Unit or cut up and sold for scrap on the site.

The United States Army

From 1951 to 1957 there were a considerable number of American army personnel stationed at Langham.

The first unit to arrive was the US Army 50th Radio Controlled Target Aircraft Detachment. This unit was equipped with large radio-controlled model aircraft known as RCATS. They would launch these aircraft from a circular roadway commonly referred to as the 'whirlygig', the remnants of which can be found on the edge of the marsh at Stiffkey. They were also launched by catapult from Weybourne. Gunners would attempt to shoot the targets down, but if they failed, the aircraft were recovered by the deployment of a parachute.

In 1953, a battalion of the 32nd Anti-Aircraft Artillery Brigade arrived. They were equipped with the Skysweeper, a 75mm automatic radar-operated anti-aircraft gun which was fired for the first time in Europe at Weybourne in August 1954. Personnel from this unit were billeted on the site, on the east side of the Morston road.

Within this battalion there was a meteorological section that deployed hydrogen filled balloons from Weybourne. These balloons measured the wind speed at high altitudes, as well as the humidity and temperatures, all of which could affect the flight of the shells from the Skysweeper guns. The information was fed into a computer and the gun then adjusted accordingly.

In 2011 a member of this detachment who served at Langham in 1956, Larry Anderson from Minnesota, returned to retrace his old haunts.

Weybourne

He who would old England win
Must at Weybourne Hoop begin.

Invasion by our enemies has been faced many times throughout history at Weybourne, beginning with the Danes, whose king threatened to land at "Waborne Stone" and fight a battle in which blood would run to Cromer ridge.

Later, invasion plans of a French king marked out the waters of Weybourne Hoop as a place to come ashore.

Later still, beacon fires were prepared as a lookout for the expected Spanish Armada.

World War One brought the fear of a German invasion and lines of defences were prepared surrounding the area. Miles of trenches were dug alongside the Glaven River, from the coast inland to Stody, and regiments of infantry horsemen stood by in each village. Thousands of poppies covered the newly dug soil. In 1940 again the deep Weybourne waters were thought to be one of the most likely landing places for Hitler's troops. Lines of pillboxes replaced the trenches, and inland, massive 9:2in howitzers were ranged onto the beaches. Military camps abounded in all directions.

RAF Weybourne

Probably the smallest airfield in Great Britain during the Second World War, RAF Weybourne was situated on the edge of the north Norfolk coast just west of Sheringham, close to the village of Weybourne.

Its use was associated with the Royal Artillery Anti Aircraft practice camp close by. The site was first active during the 1930s, when Queen Bee radio-controlled target aircraft were launched by catapult for use by RA Territorial Regiments during their annual summer camps.

During one of the summer camps at Weybourne a number of high ranking German Air Force Officers were guests. On another occasion the huge German airship, The Graf Zeppelin, flew over the camp.

The Queen Bee was essentially a DH Tiger Moth, a two seat single engine biplane - an elementary training aircraft. It was a specially built version equipped so that it could be flown by radio control without a pilot, although it could also be flown in the normal way by a pilot if need be. It was fitted with twin floats so it could be landed on water. Over four hundred were built.

Operations with the aircraft were limited to good weather conditions as their flight, and especially landing on water, had to be visible to the ground radio operator for most of the time.

When the weather was unsuitable for the Queen Bees, Henleys from Bircham Newton would tow drogue targets for the guns.

The Queen Bee units were based at RAF Henlow from where they flew out to the various RA training camps during the summer months (April to September), returning to Henlow again for the winter. The camps included Weybourne, Watchet, Manobier and Bude.

At Weybourne facilities were very basic with small bell tents for accommodation and a marquee for the dining room. There was also a small canvas hangar, a small cookhouse building and an orderly room hut.

The aircraft catapult was situated at the far right of the site at the top of a steep slope which lead down to the beach. There was no actual landing strip; any flying done by the Queen Bees and a Magister was from the open field.

One of the airmen at the 1939 camp was Don Campion who remembers the CO as being Squadron/Ldr. Carter, who had a large hospital-type tent for his accommodation. There were also two junior officers, P/O Anthony and a New Zealand P/O.

In conjunction with the unit an RAF motor launch was based at Wells, coxed by Cpl. Wheel, known as 'Harpy'. After each firing session, providing the Queen Bee survived, it would be landed on the water close to the launch and then towed back to Wells quay for dismantling, and returned to Weybourne by road transport. Standard wheels would then be fitted for air tests.

When war was declared in September 1939 the tents were hastily camouflaged and a blackout enforced.

On 6 January 1941 a new unit, 'T' Flight, was formed at the HQ of No. 1 AACU based at Farnborough and on 3 February the main party moved up to Weybourne. This was a much larger unit than had ever previously been based there.

Commanded by a Wing/Cdr. Ovenden, it comprised some 120 officers, NCOs and airmen. Conditions were reported as somewhat primitive.

The station HQ was set up on the ground floor of Carvel Farmhouse. The officers and NCOs were billeted upstairs. The airmen were accommodated in a large old wooden hut brought over by the Army. The farm kitchen was the cook house and the water supply was a 200 gallon tank mounted on a lorry with the only hot water coming from a 15 gallon outside portable boiler. The old pre-war ablutions and earth latrines were re-opened. The farm barn became the workshops, a wooden hut was scrounged from the RAF at Bircham Newton for use as the M/T office. A hangar and aircraft catapult were erected. The grass landing strip was extended because at first it was thought that land based operations were best since the catapult could only be used in fine weather. Both systems were eventually used.

This time the recovery vessel was a small civilian coaster, the SS Radstock, from Watchett in Somerset. Captained by Eric Morse, she was based at Wells quay. This series of operations was to provide targets for trials of new secret anti-aircraft rocket projectile weapons.

During early April the Duke of Gloucester was present for the first demonstration.

A wheeled Queen Bee was launched which disappeared in a near vertical climb and was never seen again.

On the night of 24/25 May 1941 an He 111 dropped four 250kg bombs on the site, one being only 10 yards from the farm house. Luckily all failed to explode.

At the end of the month the AOC No. 70 Group, Air Commodore Cole Hamilton, who was accompanied by W/Cdr. Unwin, came to see a special demonstration of the firing of the Ack-Ack rocket weapon.

This was a rehearsal for the demonstrations held on 6 June 1941 when the Prime Minister, Sir Winston Churchill, and a large distinguished company, including the Chief of Air Staff, came to Weybourne to see a rocket firing demonstration.

V4797 Queen Bee was flown over at 400 feet. 160 missiles were fired but the aircraft appeared not to be hit and landed safely on the water.

The Prime Minister and his party had lunch in the Officers' Mess at the Army camp. After lunch bad weather and lack of time prevented further firing.

It was decided on this day to erect an airmen's dining hall on the site. The facilities of a small NAAFI were also now available in part of a wooden hut.

A few days later further trials took place when V4755 Queen Bee flew at 5,000 and 9,000 feet for two hours. Ninety rockets were fired at the aircraft but no hits were made. During the afternoon session P4780 was the target at 2,000 feet. This time a number of hits were made.

So now with new encouragement, the Prime Minister was invited back for another look which took place on 18 June 1941. V4797 was launched and after three quarters of an hour a near hit put the aircraft out of control.

Later in the afternoon L5894 was launched. After forty minutes of rocket firing she was still airborne so Army Bofors guns were brought into action to finally put her into the sea. Both the aircraft brought down on this day were later salvaged from the sea and taken to Wells quay for collection by 54 MU.

The flight continued to provide target facilities for Weybourne camp for the next ten months.

During September 1941 the AOC made another visit to discuss plans to enlarge the base. Work commenced to build a signals section with cipher office and radio room, but suddenly in May 1942 orders were given to close the site and disband the flight. Within a few days all the equipment had gone. The CO was posted to HQ Flying Training Command. On 30 May the last Queen Bee left for Langham; on 8 June the hangar was dismantled and sent to 3 MU and the last man, F/Lt G. Wallas, closed the station on 30 July 1941. He was posted to 41 OTU.

Later after the end of the war, further specialised units were based at Weybourne including both British and American PTA (Pilotless Target Aircraft) units and RAF Radar. Military helicopters have visited the site on various exercises and in recent years an airstrip has been available for use by light civil aircraft whose occupants wished to visit the Muckleburgh Collection.

What was the fate of the Queen Bees?

V4743 Shot downWeybourne 22 Apr 41

V4755 Shot down Weybourne 2 July 41

V4757 Crashed on launching Weybourne 5 May 41

V4767 Shot down Cromer 16 Sep 41

V4797 Shot down Weybourne 18 Jun 42

V4799 Shot down Weybourne 3 Aug 41

V4751 Crashed on landing Weybourne 26 Mar 42

L5894 Shot down Weybourne 18 Jun 41

L7760 Crashed into the sea Weybourne 8 Apr 41

N1844 Spun into the sea Weybourne 27 Jun 39

N1846 Shot down Weybourne 2 Aug 39

N1847 Crashed into the sea Weybourne 5 Jul 39

P4780 Hit by AA fire Weybourne June 41

Other Crashes and Accidents, at Langham (unless stated otherwise).

Tiger Moth N6719 1 AACU Weybourne

Crashed into the sea off Weybourne crew drowned. 30 Jan 42.

Henley L3386 1 AACU Langham.

Lost in fog short of fuel, landed RAF Weybourne. 22 Dec 41. Later flown out after removal of winch and other heavy equipment.

Tiger Moth DE166 Langham station flight.

Crashed near Stiffkey.

RAF Langham crash vehicle crashed on way to the incident. One fireman killed. 25 Jun '42.

Tiger Moth W7954 1 AACU Langham.

Crashed into the fuel storage depot, Langham,on take off. 12 Nov '42.

Henley L3243 1 AACU Langham.

Hit airfield grass cutter on take off, grass cutter driver killed. 2 May '42.

9.8.44 Beaufighter NT958, 455 Squadron

Crashed near Langham.

24.8.44 Beaufighter NE326, 455 Squadron

Crashed into building on approach after engine trouble.

30.9.44 Warwick BV308, 280 Squadron

Forced landed on mud flats Warham after engine failure, crew OK.

18.3.45 Wellington NC623, 612 Squadron

Bombs exploded after fire in fuel bowser aircraft destroyed.

18.3.45 Wellington PF820, 612 Squadron

Destroyed by above.

26.3.45 Wellington NB824, 524 Squadron
Crashed after engine failure on take off.

26.3.45 Wellington ND133, 612 Squadron
Belly landed return ops.

5.5.45 Wellington NC513, 407 Squadron
Crashed after overshoot.

11.5.45 Wellington LP404, 24 OUT
Crashed onto barn in village after engine failure after overshoot.

5.10.45 Hurricane LF371, 521 Squadron
Hit radio mast, crashed.

12.3.46 Hurricane PZ817, 1402 Flight
Crashed while making forced landing at Stiffkey.

26.4.46 Beaufighter RD501, 254 Squadron
Collided with building after brakes failure.

26.4.46 Beaufighter RD502, 254 Squadron
Crashed Hindringham.

23.7.53 Spitfire TB747, 2 CAACU
Hit ground in failure to pull out of dive.

12.8.53 Mosquito TH997, 2 CAACU
Belly landing after engine cut out on take off.

18.2.57 Mosquito TK605, 2 CAACU
U/c leg collapsed landing.

13.3.57 Mosquito RV367, 2 CAACU
U/c leg collapsed landing.

Some Memories of RAF Langham

Because of its distance from any large town, entertainment for personnel had to be mainly home-made. During 1944/45 there was no shortage of talent on the base. A very successful dance band was formed led by Ken Humphreys, also a musical concert party which gave performances on the camp and for villages nearby. One revue show presented by them had these names in the cast: Murrell Askew, Connie Bellenger, Gill Boswell, Dorothy Clark, Beryl Hollyfield, Helen Morris, Ted Barratt, Frank Dobby, Jim Freelove, Jim Hart, Ernie Pratt, Ian Humphries, Len Longland, Winnie Williams, Andy Morrell, Sid Small, Smokie Simpson, Joe Steadman, Sid Walker, Jock Paul, John Kinniburgh, and Don Speight. How many were to continue in show business after being demobbed?

The village pub in Langham, 'The Bluebell', brought a touch of home to many of the personnel, and is remembered, above all else, in many of their memoirs.

For some, there were sorties to pubs in other villages, such as Cley, Binham, etc.

The official RAF Cycle was useful for visits to Holt pictures and the chip shop.

The nearest railway station for the base was Thursford, about five miles away, on the Fakenham to Melton Constable line.

Holt station was about the same distance and may have been used by some, but official postings etc, would have been to and from Thursford.

Harry Smith
Cooking at Langham Hall 1941/42

From Bircham Newton I was sent on detachment to Langham with about thirty other personnel. We were billeted in Langham Hall in the centre of the village. I was airman, general duties, and spent my entire time working in the Hall kitchen. Most of the cooking was done on a large old coal fired range in the main kitchen. In another room there was a smaller Aga-type stove which we also used. There were some Sawyer stoves outside in the Hall yard; these contraptions were run on coal dust doused with paraffin. Sometimes they worked and sometimes not.

My jobs consisted of preparing the dining room, cutting up bread and cake, carting coal, stoking the fires and filling the water tanks. The water came from a well and was pumped up by a hand pump. A lead indicator hung down from the ceiling and this was carefully watched to see when pumping was needed.

Stoking the fires caused a considerable amount of coal dust and soot which got into all our food supplies.

I became more and more involved in the actual cooking and I was often the night duty cook, supplying tea and sandwiches for the airfield night duty crews and also starting to prepare the breakfast. The bacon was started at 6am in the Aga and when partially done it was transferred to the cool oven to finish.

The rations arrived daily from Bircham. The exact requirements for the next 24 hours were sent, so we had no stocks of food.

This sometimes caused great difficulty when the breakfast menu was beans on toast. The beans arrived as dried haricot beans which required 24 hours soaking before use and with the meal being just 12 hours away, this meant problems; so we put the beans and other vegetables through a hand mincing machine to make them edible! Alas on one occasion this system also accounted for the loss of the end of one of the cook's fingers; this we were unable to find before the meal was served, but we had no complaints! I moved from the Hall to quarters in some tiny cottages opposite, just one room up and one down, but about ten personnel slept in each.

We had a corporal cook who was keen with a gun. He would go off on his motor cycle, with the gun down his trouser leg, returning with game for the larder.

Wells had a good fish and chip shop run by a local fisherman. There was also another in Blakeney in a large building with trestle tables and benches set out.

Trevor Morgan (8524 SE)
Langham Village Wimpy Crash

On 11th May 1945 we had just returned from our usual visit to the flicks in Holt and were back in the billet where I was engaged in one of my frequent arguments with LAC Batey. Suddenly we heard a Wimpy flying overhead. You could always tell a Wimpy, they made a distinctive whistling sound. Batey said "That aircraft is in trouble!" and I said "No, it's just an old OTU training aircraft with de-rated engines." They flew on 87 octane petrol and so sounded different. As we argued about that, the lights in the billet flickered. We all rushed outside in time to see the Wimpy with its landing lights on, coming down on the village. We jumped on our bikes and set out to look for it.

We arrived at the cross roads where a crowd had already gathered. The plane had apparently hit the wireless mast, scraped the Church tower, scattering debris into the road and then demolished one side of the barn on the other side of the road. This barn was being used as a canteen, but was luckily now shut. It then slid along and slewed across the entrance to the WAAF site and came to rest with its tail against a tree.

Jock Marshall had apparently been first on the scene, his cycle had as usual broken down outside the WAAF site. He must have been very close to the crash when it occurred.

Most of the crew luckily were able to get out of the wreck unaided, but Jock had pulled the pilot out.

When we arrived the crew were getting into the ambulance. The captain was dazed but demanded to be allowed to stand on his own. He joined the others in the ambulance which left, but

then he realised the rear gunner was missing so he insisted on returning to the crash.

The rear gunner of an aircraft making a crash landing would often, contrary to the approved drill, remain in his turret turning it so that he could get out of the aircraft in case of fire. In this case the turret had become detached and could not be found. It was now very dark and as usual at a crash site there was a good deal of noise. Gyros continued to whirr, air to escape and the wreckage to creak and groan, and there was a strong smell of oil and petrol.

Chiefy Tyson took charge telling everyone to douse their fags and search for the missing gunner. In an outhouse at the end of the barn we found the turret jammed up in the roof beams. Chiefy and a couple of lads climbed up and got the gunner out but he was dead on arrival at sick bay. I believe the crew were Canadians.

This brief history is intended as a reminder of the time when the airfield at Langham was in daily operational use, to bring back memories to those who served there and to those who lived in the area at the time and also to inform others of what life was like then. We must also remember all those who lost their lives while stationed at RAF Langham.

Post script: The rear gunner was Flying Officer (Air Gunner) Glen James Hay from Loon Lake, Saskatchewan, Canada. He is buried in the Brookwood Military Cemetery, near Woking, Surrey.

British Empire Medal citation: Leading Aircraftwoman Ivy Cross

On the night of 25th March 1945, a heavily loaded Wellington aircraft crashed and burst into flames near the airfield shortly after taking off for operations. Leading Aircraftwoman Cross drove her van across several fields to reach the scene of the crash. She helped to drag clear several of the crew who had been thrown out of the aircraft although ammunition and explosives were detonating at very close quarters. Once they were clear of the flames she rendered first aid to the injured. Owing to the intense heat she was unable to approach the aircraft again in order to try to rescue other trapped airmen. She returned to her station of duty at Flying Control and shortly after arriving there another Wellington aircraft crashed on the edge of the airfield. Leading Aircraftwoman Cross was first on the scene with her van. Most of the crew members were able to get clear of the wreckage, but the rear gunner was trapped. She assisted in smashing the rear turret and in helping the rear gunner to safety. She then rendered first aid and helped members of the crew to sick quarters

Leading Aircraftwoman Cross has attended fourteen crashes and on twelve occasions has helped members of the aircrew from crashed and burning aircraft. She has shown outstanding courage and complete disregard for her own safety.

LEFT: *Leading Aircraftwoman Ivy Cross BEM.*
RIGHT: *Flying Officer (Air Gunner) Glen James Hay.*